MW01610592

THE LITTLE BOOK OF
INSPIRATION

DANNY BROWN

MORNING RAIN
PUBLISHING

The Little Book of Inspiration

By
Danny Brown

Copyright 2015 by Danny Brown
Cover design copyright 2015 by Morning Rain Publishing

ISBN: 978-1-928133-70-4

Print Edition 2016

Dedication

To my beautiful wife, Jaclyn,
and my wonderful children, Ewan and Salem.
You inspire me to be better every single day.

Acknowledgements

To the dreamers who push for a better day
for all—never stop.

And to the Morning Rain team, who took a chance
on a little book like this.

Contents

Yesterday Mortality Caught Up With Me

Yesterday, my beautiful daughter turned two.

Like all children that age, she had a wonderful party attended by family and friends, ate lots of cake, ripped open carefully wrapped presents without a care in the world, and generally had the carefree party that children of that age have.

It reminded me of my own mortality.

I had kids late in life. Today, I'm forty-five—my daughter is two, my son will be four in May. My wife is thirty-two.

Because I'm an older dad (and, I guess, an older husband), I find myself thinking more about the future than perhaps I should.

How I'll technically be a pensioner when my kids are at University.

How I'll be in my fifties at my kids' school sports days, and probably let them down in the parent/children events where there's any kind of competitive edge needed.

How I may die, leaving them as young adults, without ever having the chance to impart any learning I have accrued over the years of my own life that may set them in good stead for the years ahead of them.

But you know what? I can't be sad.

To be sad is to avoid the experiences and the memories I've already had with them, and those yet to come.

To be sad is to believe that all their "alive moments" will stop if I can no longer share them.

To be sad is to be alone.

And I can never be alone, because even writing this I can see the faces of my wife and my kids, and that makes me smile. If I can see them now in my conscious, perhaps I can see them in my unconscious too.

Yesterday, mortality may have caught up with me. Today, I welcomed it as a future friend who will help me remember the present.

The Religion of Humanity

I've never been much of a religious man, yet I celebrate Christmas. I celebrate Easter.

In days past, depending on who I was with, and where I was, I celebrated Hanukkah with Jewish friends, Yule in Scandinavia, the Seven Principles of Kwanzaa in the United States, and Ramadan with Muslim friends.

As much as I celebrated these different events, my friends and the people they introduced me to, also celebrated other festivals, including ones that (technically) went against their beliefs.

Religion is often blamed as the cause for the world's woes and—often—it can be.

Yet, for all the wrongs religion can foster, it can also enable the greatest celebration of all—the religion of humanity.

We have one shot at this thing we call life. We can either embrace it—and embrace those we share the moment with, of all creeds and religions—or we can let it destroy us, and those we could do so much more with.

Religion is multi-faceted. I get that. I'm not naive enough to think we can all overcome our differences in belief, whatever they may be, overnight.

But imagine how much we could achieve if we believed in the religion of humanity a little bit more than we do…

Danny Brown

Watched From Below

One of my favourite quotes by the late martial artist Bruce Lee focuses on how "non-believers watch from below".

The gist of the quote is to show that you will always have doubters, but that doesn't matter because these doubters will be watching from below as you soar.

It speaks so much to our own lives, where we hear the doubters every day, at every step of our growth. How our dreams are just that, and reality is a different beast we'll never tame if our heads remain in the clouds.

And maybe that's true. Maybe the dreams we have are the unattainable kind.

But wouldn't it be nice to find out on our own terms?

Danny Brown

Building Creativity

It doesn't matter if it's for blogging, painting, making movies, taking pictures, writing, or whatever—make time every day.

Even if it's five minutes, make time.

Take a picture.

Write a blog post.

Shoot something on your video camera.

You don't have to publish it—just get into the habit of doing it and learning your trade.

You'll be surprised at how you grow, both in creativity and in the strength to make your creation public.

Danny Brown

The World Might Actually Be Okay

Sometimes, when reading the news, it feels like the world is on a downward spiral. Ignorance, hate, bigotry, and pointless tragic deaths.

But then... then we have stories like the San Francisco Batkid. The city of San Francisco worked with the Make a Wish Foundation to turn the city into a replica of Batman's Gotham City for a day, to make the wish of a five year old cancer patient come true. The day included rescuing citizens in danger, as well as combating Batman's arch enemies like The Penguin and Riddler. The pictures of little Miles, the kid at the heart of it all, told you what it meant to him.

Or we read about the hundreds of strangers who turned up for a lonely old soldier's funeral. Harold Jellicoe Percival died in a nursing home in November 2013; he had no friends or family to put him to rest. When an Internet campaign put the word out about this fallen hero after the local paper placed an advert, more than 300 people responded to pay their respects to someone who had given so much.

Or find out about the folks living in comfort using reverse psychology to raise money for the homeless. Volunteers from The Passage, a UK organization, held signs to share the same message a homeless person would use—except this message came from someone who was fortunate and clearly wasn't homeless. The result was an increase in donations by 25% and more than 650,000 people learned about the work The Passage does and why homelessness is something we can all do something about.

And you know... It makes you remember that, at the end of the day, the world might actually be okay. Here's to the good people.

Because We Never Failed

As children, we have unbridled aspirations.

We dream to be astronauts. We dream to be explorers. We dream to be princesses. We dream to be the world's greatest sports star. *We dream.*

Looking back at our childhood dreams, we rarely feel we failed because we didn't become the astronaut. Or marry the prince. Or found new lands. Or had stadiums cheering our name.

Instead, we look back and remember a time when dreams had no limits and anything was possible, even if, in reality, it never was.

Yet, we never use the *fail* word. Because, in truth, we never failed.

Just because something didn't happen doesn't mean it's a failure. Far from it.

That failed astronaut? Perhaps he became a doctor and found a cure for cancer.

That failed princess? Perhaps she became a politician and ended global hunger.

That failed sports star? Perhaps he became an author and wrote the book that changed the world forever.

Failure is simply a word. A perception of what might have been versus what is. Another path on an ongoing journey. Something that exists because we allow it to.

If we allow failure to exist, we can also disallow it. And

if we disallow it, we can think the way we did as children. Where one dream not realized becomes another dream still to happen.

Because if something can still happen, it hasn't failed. And if failure hasn't yet happened? Then perhaps it never will.

It Just Happens

We don't come into this world knowing what to do next. It just happens.

Our first steps. Our first words. Our first grazed knee. Our first illness. Our first loss. Our first crush.

We're tenants in a short-term lease. All these firsts have the potential to be our lasts within the same breath.

Often, because of that, we try to force things to go the way we feel they should, as opposed to letting them go the way they should to make us really *feel*.

And that's the funny thing about all the best there is in life. It just happens.

Enjoy it.

Danny Brown

Failure IS An Option

One of the most famous quotes in living memory is, *"Failure is not an option."* (*Apollo 13*. Universal Studios. 1998. Film)

While the quote may make for great movie fodder, in reality failure is an option in many circumstances, and should be celebrated as such.

Without failing in early "love", we'd never meet the person of our real dreams.

Without failing in our original career path, we'd never find the one we were truly meant for.

Without failing at outrageous goals when we knew no better, we'd never meet the realistic ones when we matured to better knowledge.

It's hard to fail. It hurts. But it would hurt even more if we weren't where we are now because we did fail.

Failure is another word for a long-term success plan. Much like the magic that can happen because we never failed, the same magic can happen when we *do* fail. Perhaps even more so—all you have to do is be willing to try.

Danny Brown

The Beauty of Silence

As someone who loves to blog, I'm a fairly active person on the web. Indeed, many of the stories of inspiration you're reading stemmed from a blog project I used to have. Whenever I have a spare moment, I'm thinking of topics for my blogs and how they can relate to the message I want to share.

For a while, when my work required travelling during the week, I deliberately didn't post anything on the various blog channels I manage

My marketing blog stayed quiet. My photography blog stayed quiet. My book blog stayed quiet. Even the social networks I'm on remained quiet as I paused from updating them.

Instead, I preferred to switch off and concentrate on family time for that week.

Usually, mornings and evenings are times dedicated to the family. Because I'd miss two days of this special time, it made sense to give my family more time the days I was home.

It was heavenly.

Sometimes you need to switch off and appreciate the beauty of silence. Even if that silence is the sound of two kids under five going a little bit nutty around the house...

Danny Brown

If I Were to Die Tomorrow

Would my son remember the dad who rewarded the times he did good deeds, or the dad who told him off for the infrequent times he was naughty?

Would my daughter remember the dad who tickled her so, or the dad who made her cry by saying no to the things that could hurt her?

Would my wife remember the man who loved her from the very first day he knew her, or the ass who could sometimes forget?

Would the friends I want to support more than anything remember the one time I couldn't?

We make decisions that change the world every day. We may not see the results, but does that mean they never existed?

The ratios are always in the balance—how they pan out is up to us.

Danny Brown

We Are All We Have

We're born with our eyes closed, and we leave with our eyes closed.

In-between, for however long we're on this planet, our eyes are open. Yet, sometimes, it feels like they've stayed closed since our first breath in the open air.

We see colour, but we see it as something that makes people different and not in a good way.

We see love, but it's the wrong kind of love if it's between people of the same sex.

We see beliefs, but we rip them down and start wars to force our own beliefs on others.

We see so many things that are beautiful, but we taint them with our own twisted vision of what's beautiful.

But we are all we have.

If only we opened our eyes, we would see that we are all the same.

We live; we love; we laugh; we cry. We experience the same pain when our loved ones die. We experience the same joy when a new child is born. At our very core, we are all the same.

We are all we have. More than that, though, **we are all we need.**

It's time to open our eyes to that.

Danny Brown

The Best Advice

People are full of best advice. When we need a little push in a certain direction, or guidance on why we should do one thing but not another, we rarely have a shortage of voices offering their wisdom.

This can be both a good and bad thing.

Good, in that the advice is usually helpful in enabling us to make the right decision. For example, the favourite piece of advice ever given to me was from my granddad, who said, "Always stand up before you flush."

A little esoteric, maybe, but you have to admit, the man had a point!

Sometimes, though, advice can put us off a path that actually turns out to be the right one. That's not to say it's deliberate on the part of those giving you the advice. Friends may tell you to move on from a broken relationship, for example, when all the relationship needed was a moment apart to be perfect again.

They may feel they're doing you a favour, when what they're really doing is holding you back from true happiness and satisfaction. All in the name of advice.

The best advice? Listen to your trusted circles, but realize that—at the end of the day—there's only one person who will ever live your life.

You've managed to get yourself to this point so far, so you must be doing something right.

Listen to yourself more. You may be pleasantly surprised.

Danny Brown

Wishful Thinking

We spend too much time wishing things were different, but sometimes we need to see the great things we already have because things *aren't* different.

Danny Brown

Footprints in the Sand

Footprints in the sand are fleeting—a transient snapshot in time that disappear when the tide comes in. Even the footprints that are further in eventually become invisible alongside a million others.

But for that moment in time, they're physical. They're proof that you did something.

That you existed.

Some folks might say that footprints in the sand don't matter *because* they wash away. That no matter how you spin it, the lack of physical proof of you having left your footprint means it's only your word that you ever walked there in the first place.

But they're missing the bigger picture.

Even when the tide washes away your footprint, it's taking the sand that supported your print to another shore. The grains mix with a new beach, and your old footprints mix with new ones left by new people.

People you'll more than likely never meet, but people whose lives you're now a part of.

Your sand is now their sand.

The same goes for that sand of yours that didn't get washed away, but instead mixed with the footsteps of others. You become part of their existence. The moment your grain mixes with their grain, you've shared a mutual moment.

In essence, you've touched someone's life without even knowing it.

Now. Transfer that to what you're doing now.

Your blog. Your business. Your job. Your employees. Your friends. Your colleagues. Your connections. Your words.

Your actions.

Every day we have the opportunity to touch people's lives without knowing it. Every day we have a chance to improve a mood without knowing it. Every day we have a chance to **make a difference**.

All we need to do is leave some footprints in the sand. Ready to walk?

How Change and Persistent Vision Can Help You Find What Matters to You

In his book *Tribes*, Seth Godin talks about Chris Sharma, an American rock climber who forever changed the way climbers looked at scaling a cliff. Instead of the normal left-right, left-right approach of hand over hand, Sharma jumps (known as a dyno).

It's a leap of faith at its purest, since a fall while rock-climbing can be a long way down.

Seth's analogy is that because of Sharma's vision, the status quo needn't be the norm, and experimenting with how far you can push the limitations of the dyno can lead to life-changing results. Other climbers experimented, and soon the dyno wasn't the exception anymore.

Finding Your Dyno.

Persistent vision is difficult. Persistence in itself is tough. Much like a rock climber, you need stamina. Stamina to see something through—to reach the endgame. Like rocks that jut out, obstacles will stand in your way. And the more persistent your vision, the more frequent and tougher the obstacles will be.

That's why it's called persistence. That's why you need to reach out and find your dyno and push it to its limits. That's why you need to take your leap of faith and trust in the safety of your landing.

Change doesn't happen overnight, **but it does happen**.

The Story of Persistent Vision

At the tail end of 2008, I had a vision. The idea was simple enough—pick 12 charities and raise $12,000 per charity, with a different charity being featured every month of the year. This idea became the 12for12k project.

It was maybe a little ambitious and perhaps a little crazy. But it was something I knew could work and believed in one hundred percent. And when I believe in something, I'm persistent to the end.

I didn't know if my vision would work. I didn't know if people would share it, or whether I'd be the lonely guy with a plan and a road map that no one wanted to read. Thankfully, though, people did. Then more people. And when obstacles got in the way, the persistence that had started in me had also started in others, and they barged their way through the obstacles.

They jumped their dynos.

Just over twelve months later, a group of persistent people with a shared vision had raised over $91,000 for charity (which broke $100,000 in January 2010), and set out their stalls for future dynos to come.

Endgame and Beginnings

This isn't a story about ego. This is a story about how you have the same persistence in you, too. How you have the same visions for what matters to you. How you can find your dyno and leapfrog it every single time.

Afraid to start blogging? Write the first word then leave it. Then go back and write another. Then leave it. Go back. Leave. Persist. Jump your dyno—the blog will happen.

Afraid to start your own business? Buy the first product. Store it. Buy another. Store it. Scour the classifieds. Buy another product. Find the audience, write a short advert (could be that first blog post). Persist. Build slowly. Let your stamina feed your persistence and jump your dyno.

The point is, change *is* waiting for you. Persistence doesn't mean overnight. Change doesn't happen overnight.

But it does happen.

Ready to jump *your* dyno?

Danny Brown

The Passion of Anger

Abraham Lincoln once said:

"You can tell the greatness of a man by what makes him angry."

Taking that a little step further, I'd add:

Anger drives you to seek a solution; passion drives you to see it through.

How about you—passion or anger?

Danny Brown

The Choices We Make

The choices we make reveal the true nature of our character.

Danny Brown

The Beauty of the Printed Word

"A room without books is like a body without a soul."—
Marcus Tullius Cicero.

With the proliferation of digital readers, tablets, and smartphone apps to read books today, you might wonder why anyone would still want to buy a printed book.

Perhaps, the question should be what benefit you get from reading a printed book.

Like the shared moment a stranger on a train notices your book cover and asks you about its contents.

Or that crispness of a newly purchased book and the first turn of its virgin pages.

Or the wondrous gaze of a child the first time they step into a library lined floor to ceiling with adventures untold.

Or simply that the weathered old copy of the book your first love gave you remains in your treasured possessions the way an ebook never could.

Why buy a printed book? Why indeed.

Danny Brown

Shouldn't We All Be Like Children?

Children fear nothing. They may be scared of something, but it's a different emotion.

They want to check out everything around them. They look at things differently from us. They see unique and new; we see *"been there, done that"*.

Children have an innocence that says everything has yet to be discovered. They don't care about the safe, the boring— they want fresh and exciting. They see the world through the eyes of someone who doesn't know the meaning of the words, *"too far"* or *"some other time"*.

Shouldn't we all be like children? In life, in love, in business? Does our fear of real life stop us from overcoming everything that's holding back our true success?

I think I'd like to be a child. How about you?

Danny Brown

The Only Difference is Opportunity and Realization

Often in life, we look and compare to who and what we see, and believe we'll never reach that plateau. It could be a higher positioned job, a better seat at the game, or a newer car in the driveway.

We believe we'll never reach that because clearly we're not good enough to do so, otherwise we'd be there now, right?

Wrong.

The difference is opportunity and realization. Opportunity can be overcome—the right moment, the right contact, the right decision.

Realization, though, is the deal breaker. Realizing you *are* good enough and *can* get there is where everything begins to happen.

You just need to realize it.

Danny Brown

The Commitment of Success

Being unsure is scary. It's a lot different from being sure. Instead of the safety net of knowledge, there's the daunting chasm of uncertainty. It's not easy to step from the warmth of the old to the chill of the new.

The same goes for commitment.

It takes a lot to commit. Especially if you're someone who needs certain guarantees before you make the leap. Otherwise, the chequebook is staying in your pocket until the next discussion.

The problem is, while you're being unsure of commitment because of the uncertainty of success, your competitors are enjoying success because of the certainty of their commitment.

A slight difference in wording but a big difference in results.

So, what can you do?

Accept Uncertainty

Remember when you were learning to drive, and you thought you'd never get the hang of it? You couldn't get used to clutch control, or reverse parking, or even the simple ten-and-two hand position? We all did it, and we all thought the same thing.

Then there was that one pivotal lesson where everything just fell into place and the next thing we knew, we were driving. Make your uncertainty your penultimate driving lesson. Accept that not knowing everything at a given moment in time is natural. Think of how many have been in the same position as you are now, but made it through. Believe that failure this time isn't the end. No one gets it right first time; great success is built from second chances.

Uncertainty is a natural emotion when we're faced with something new. If familiarity breeds contempt, then fresh breeds caution.

There's nothing wrong with caution; it keeps us alert and ready to make changes in direction if needed. It's when we let uncertainty and caution combine that stops us from moving in the first place.

This combination can lead to the fear of commitment, but if you need success before commitment, you'll never have either.

What choice will you make?

Even Little Dogs
Can Piss on a Big Building

"Even a little dog can piss on a big building."—Jim Hightower.

As people, we're fixated on size. We want bigger houses, bigger cars, bigger offices, bigger pay cheques.

If our neighbour gets a pool, ours has to be bigger. It's one of the fallacies of being human; *big* means *successful.*

The same goes for business. We see corporations wanting bigger land, bigger deals, bigger profits, and bigger golden handshakes when the time comes for executives to move on.

In business, like in life, big means successful.

But does it?

Does a company having four thousand employees mean success? Ask Enron about that. Four thousand employees lost their jobs and their life savings following the biggest corporate fraud in history.

Does having some of the biggest names in your corner mean success? HD-DVD would suggest otherwise. Despite being backed by some of the biggest names from the world of movies and consumer electronics, the format lost out to the inferior Blu-ray and was abandoned shortly after launch.

Or how about having one of the biggest movies of the decade to build your product around? In 1982, Atari produced five million copies of their official E.T. game, which was based on the Steven Spielberg movie of the same name.

51

Rushed out to capitalize on the Christmas market, the game was a massive flop due to so many bugs caused by the rush to get the game to market, with over 3.5 million copies returned by retailers. Its commercial failure was one of the reasons behind Atari's massive fall from grace. Legend even has it that these unsold games are buried somewhere in the New Mexico desert, in an attempt to hide the scale of their failure.

So despite our innate belief that size is the measure of our success, it isn't—it's how you *use* your own size that defines success.

We work in an age where Starbucks can be in your office. Where landlines are no longer needed for our communications. Where business deals can be done thousands of miles apart with none of the attendees ever having met.

Simply put, we live in an age when perception isn't so much a factor as perception *of* perception. And this puts you in the driving seat.

You decide how you're perceived.

You define how polished you are.

You define how big you appear.

To some, big may still be the measuring stick of success—and that's fine. They'll probably be the same ones cutting costs further down the line when they realize big cheques need even bigger profits.

But for you? Big is what you make it. And if a small dog can piss on a big building, so can you.

Ready to shake a leg?

52

The Fallacy of Numbers

We get so wrapped up in numbers at times.

At Christmas, we want more presents than we got the year before—same goes for birthdays.

In high school, we want to lose our virginity at a younger age than our friends (and then have more girlfriends/boyfriends than them). Or we want to get higher scores on our tests than our fellow students, either for ourselves or to please our parents. At work, we want to get bigger raises and more recognition than our colleagues.

And yet, numbers are superficial. Do we really need the numbers on a scale to tell us we should be happy with our weight, or should we be happy for our health knowing that weight is another set of numbers to control us?

So, sure, numbers may make us feel better and enable us to have a better "life", but that depends on your definition of what a better life is. For me, it's being able to spend evening and weekend time with my wife and kids.

By all means, care about how you are perceived—just don't let the numbers rule you.

Danny Brown

Being Wrong is Okay

Most people hate to be wrong. Most people hate to admit they're wrong even more. For many people, admitting they're wrong is a sign of weakness.

Yet, it's okay to be wrong. In fact, we need to be wrong more and celebrate that fact—because it's the only way we truly grow.

Danny Brown

The Old Man and the Boy

The old man and the boy spent a lifetime sharing tales
Of days when the man was not so old, and he'd ride on the backs of whales.
The boy listened closely, held in awe, to the stories that he heard,
And when he saw the glint in the old man's eyes, the boy didn't doubt a word.
On a sandy beach the two would walk, the man's dog by their side,
Throwing pebbles out to the sea racing against the tide.
Like guardians, the two would stand with their winter coats drawn tight,
And in the summertime, round an old campfire, they'd share stories in the night.

There was love in his eyes when the old man smiled,
And the love, it was returned,
And the boy would pray there'd never be a time
When the fire no longer burned.

For it's a friendship no one can understand
And far stronger than you and I.
It's a love between two generations,
And it's far too strong to die.

For the stories passed between a grandfather
And the grandson he so loves
Builds a wall so strong you could only pass
If you flew in the skies above.

These carefree days would pass so slow, each day held something new.

Days spent fishing in the downstream flow 'neath a summer sky so blue.

The tales of the one that got away made the young boy's mother laugh,

And when the old man argued handsomely she'd cry, "Away and don't be daft!"

Yet, life is just a short-lived thing, and all things must surely end.

For death awaits us one and all around each turn and bend.

The old man passed away in wintertime, so gentle in his sleep,

And though the boy cries painfully, there are memories to keep.

Not Belonging

Often, we stay somewhere or with someone because we feel we belong.

We stay with a partner because we belong together.

We stay at a company because we belong at that place.

We stay with a circle of friends because we belong in that group.

Yet, often, we confuse belong with habit. Instead of truly belonging, we remain somewhere, or with someone, because the habit has formed and we feel we know no better.

Because of that, we miss opportunities that present themselves that could make our lives infinitely better and richer. To miss out on these opportunities would be truly sad.

Just because you're somewhere doesn't mean you belong there.

Danny Brown

The Evolution of You

Look at your life. Personally or professionally—both tie into each other anyway, so you can look at both. How are you evolving?

How are you taking what you learn and changing what you're doing? How are you using the time you have to fill the time you have left? Are you using it, or are you abusing it?

We all have a limited shelf life—there are a ton of things we can do to make it as fulfilling as we want it to be. For yourself, you could:

Write a book. It's said everyone has at least one great book in them—are you writing yours? It doesn't matter if you're not a great writer; there are a ton of resources and people available that can make you better.

Achieve your business goals. A lot of people say that to really be happy in business, you need to own your own. Not necessarily—you can make your business your career at a company. Look at where you want to be in one, two, five, and ten years, and look at what you need to do to get there. Then keep pushing yourself to do so.

Be loved and love back. You don't have to be married or in a relationship to love and be loved—you can do anything to meet your love quota. Help with a charity; have a pet; be a teacher; volunteer at a food bank.

Danny Brown

You have the opportunity to offer love in so many ways without ever being with another person—are you using it?

How will *your* evolution be told?

Because We Learned

As children, we're unafraid to take risks.

We see the world as one big adventure, and if we hurt ourselves along the way we shed some tears, get a kiss from our parent(s), and move onto the next adventure.

Risks allows us to grow, because we know not to make the same mistake that hurt us in the first place.

Unfortunately, as adults, it seems like we've forgotten the art of learning from our mistakes.

We stay with abusive partners, we accept shit from our boss instead of looking for a job where we're valued, and we never take action on that one big idea we have because everyone will think it's stupid.

The thing is, we became the adults we are *because* we learned from our mistakes as children. And we turned out all right (mostly). There's something to be said for that, no?

Don't be afraid to take risks—you're only hurting yourselves if you don't.

Danny Brown

Ripples of Hope

We all have differing opinions. We all choose our guy over the other. We all believe our way is the best way forward.

In life. In love. In politics. In existing.

In hindsight, we realize our beliefs don't always hold sway. Sometimes—oftentimes—the other guy, the other love, the other point of view, is the right one.

Because the other guy has no agenda, no hidden message, no ulterior motive other than offering ripples of hope.

Something we can all aim for.

Danny Brown

NeverLand

There's a place that I go between sleep and the dawn
Where the moon shares the sky with the sun
And the night is ablaze with the light of the stars
And the shadows, they flicker and run.

And the sounds that you hear from the towns all around
Are of laughter and peace and of joy.
And of songs from an age where innocence yet lives
In the eyes of each girl and each boy.

And the wind, as it blows, catches each wisp of your hair
And paints pictures the width of your face.
It's a world from a time when the ships still set sail
To take you to a magical place.

And as years take my time and as lines etch my face
I know this land's still the one thing that's true.
For I just close my eyes and my heart takes me there
Where I walk, hand in hand, loving you.

So if dreams do come true and they're not just for sleep
Then I know where my NeverLand can be found.
It's being next to you and hearing you breathe
To me, that's the most magical sound.

Danny Brown

Unfostering Weakness

None of us like to admit we're weak. None of us like to present the potential of fear to our opponents, always waiting in the wings for us to slip up.

And yet... our opponents are just as fearful. Just as cautious. Just as secretive and unwilling to admit to weaknesses, too. Sometimes they hide it better, sometimes not.

But why fear weakness? Weakness isn't a bad thing.

We're told it is—by teachers, by lovers, by bosses.

Instead of highlighting our weakness and where we can improve, they should be concentrating on our strengths and where we can use them.

We should be concentrating on our strengths and allowing others in to be the blankets for our supposed failings. Because, in all honesty, our only failing, or weakness, is in allowing others to foster it.

Open up your weakness; acknowledge your strength.

You might be surprised at the results.

Danny Brown

Impossible Possibilities

Until 1519, we thought the earth was flat. Until the Wright Brothers showed otherwise in 1903, we thought it was impossible for man to fly. Until the 1940's, we still thought that steam power was the way to travel by train. As of 1968, we hadn't put a man on the moon.

Every day we're faced with impossibilities. We're told, "You can't do that; it'll never work."

But you know... an impossibility is simply a problem that we haven't conquered, yet. Consider that on your next commute to work on your electric train.

Danny Brown

Think Bigger

Take a moment to ask yourself these two questions:

- *How are we encouraging hope in those around us?*
- *How are we helping to grow the leaders of tomorrow?*

Like it or not, we're all acting in a role of leadership with every action we do.

Our reactions to situations and people around us shape the mindset of today's kids—tomorrow's leaders. We swear; they swear. We smoke; they smoke. We do drugs; they do drugs. If we're not setting the example, how can we expect our kids to?

How we work with colleagues dictates how we lead our workforce. Even if we're not managers, we're part of a decision-making process that defines that company's culture and success. Work smart, work intelligently, work respectfully.

Our voices define our outlook. Disagree with something or someone by all means, but respect their view to differ. Religion, simple points of view, movie tastes, etc.—wouldn't it be boring if we were all the same? Make your point, but allow more than yours.

Speaking for the voiceless when words aren't enough. Actions speak louder than words—know someone who's right but afraid to say so? Say it for them—don't be a passerby when the slightest encouragement can offer so much hope.

None of us are born leaders—that takes time to cultivate.

Even then, leadership is born from respect of our peers, employers, friends, and colleagues. People earn leadership—bought leadership is just politics.

Leaders make changes that others wish for but never act on. Imagine if we encouraged everyone around us to be leaders in their own right?

The Scary Concept
of Long Term Vision

For many of us, long-term vision can be a scary concept. This is understandable because it usually means that we have to put faith in something we're doing now even though it's not showing a return until much later.

This could be our businesses, our blogs, or our budding relationship with a new lover.

It's scary, because while we believe in our hearts that everything will work out, often we get impatient for results that we can see immediately.

We want our business to be profitable right away, our blogs to have hundreds of comments, subscribers and social shares, and we want that new love to be the one and to fall in love with us so we can start living our lives together.

The problem is, very rarely is something a home run out of the gate. Instead, it takes time to get to where the real gold is.

It takes time to build something worth having.

And it takes bravery to allow the luxury of that time.

But here's the thing—big successes all failed to start with, in one way or another. Hopes and dreams all started small at one point, and they didn't suffer because of non-instant success.

You can be too. You just have to embrace the concept.

Danny Brown

Make Believe Games

Did you doodle at school as a kid? Did you play make-believe games with your friends that took you to other worlds, real and imagined? Did you have an invisible friend?

Our minds are so free as kids. We imagine anything and everything. Our creativity knows no limits, and our imagination is boundless.

When do we lose that? When does our creativity go into hiding, and we settle for the ordinary and the mundane?

Some people never lose it. Some people keep the imaginative strength of children into their adult lives. You see it around you every day.

Who would have thought you could run a car on electricity? Or hear music on the go? Or watch 3-D landscapes in a 2-D setting?

Your creativity is still inside you. You never lose it. If you look closely enough, you'll see it there underneath the surface, waiting for you to renew your acquaintance.

Go find it. Rediscover the creative part you haven't used since childhood. It can be used anywhere. Your personal life. That board meeting. That business plan. That marketing idea. That blog post. That kitchen recipe. Anywhere.

Your imagination and creativity are powerful tools. They can separate you from the crowd.

The possibilities they offer, in life and in business, are endless—the only barrier is you.

Danny Brown

Imagine If

Instead of blowing $50,000 on the staff Christmas party, companies offered employees the option of a smaller bash and donated the rest to a local charity.

Instead of sending employees on a team-building exercise in the woods, companies sent them on a team-building exercise to renovate a playground in a rundown area.

Instead of using interns from the local college, companies mixed it up a little and gave a business education to kids from lower income schools.

Instead of the lavish client lunch expenses, companies offered smaller, intimate, catered meetings and bought food for a local food bank.

Instead of the expensed company cars, companies rewarded carpooling where possible and leased the local school new buses.

Imagine if.

Danny Brown

The Baby That Shouldn't Be

Jesse James Arrigo is the baby that shouldn't be.

Before he was even born, his mother had surgery while fighting cervical cancer and was told she could never have children. A year later, Jesse was born.

In May 2012, Jesse was playing in his grandparents' backyard and fell into their pond. His mother, Kristin, found him and pulled him out of the water and began to give him CPR.

Even as he was being treated within an hour of being pulled from the pond, first by the paramedics and then the emergency crew, Jesse suffered two cardiac arrests.

He then suffered seizures, dystonia and double pneumonia, and fell into a coma. The diagnosis was not good, due to the amount of time he was under water without oxygen.

To put it bluntly, Jesse was expected to die.

The thing is, children have a wonderful way of not listening to adults and those who know better.

Doctors said Jesse would never eat unaided again. Today, he's able to swallow on his own.

Doctors said he'd never be able to speak. Today, Jesse can whoop in delight at the sound of music.

Doctors feared he'd never be able to understand the world around him. Today, Jesse can track the movement of noise and people.

And today, Jesse is at home when his world threatened to be one surrounded by hospital food and strangers.

His battle is far from over. He has to have special oxygen treatment to try to resuscitate the parts of his brain damaged by the fifty-five minutes he was without oxygen.

But it's a battle Jesse is winning every single day. Today, Jesse can shed a tear from the ducts that were meant to be destroyed.

The baby that shouldn't be is the person that *wants* to be. Here's to his victory.

Your Place in the World

Have you ever looked around you—*really* looked around you—and saw your place in the world?

It could be your place in your own particular world, or your place in the bigger picture.

It doesn't really matter—all that matters is you take that look around you and recognize your place in it.

We live in a society that changes quickly and moves even quicker. It's easy to get lost, swept away, or side-tracked. Things we meant to do yesterday we don't have a chance to do tomorrow.

We live in a world where our families are second to our jobs because industries are so frail they could be gone by the time you finish reading this. We go where the work is, and not always together.

While some things can't change, others can. So let's try to change things together.

Danny Brown

Heroes Can Be Dangerous

In times of need, we often look for heroes to guide us through, or to make sense of what we're doing. Yet heroes come in many shapes and guises. False heroes offer little except hope that isn't there. We know deep inside that these heroes are false, and yet we still follow them in the vain hope that maybe it's us that's wrong.

It isn't. And you don't need false heroes to guide you—true heroes are all around you.

They're in the eyes of the children you bear as they make their way from innocence to adulthood. They're in the parents who raised you to be who you are today. They're in the mirror, looking back at you every day. That job you hold down to feed your family. These luxuries you give up to keep a roof over the heads of your loved ones. The sacrifices you make to put a smile on the faces of those you cherish.

You're being a hero every day of your life. Realize that, and forget the false heroes—no one makes a difference like you do.

Danny Brown

Pay It Forward

The world is changing. The greedy are being found out for who, and what, they are, and the society changers are coming to the fore. Be part of this.

Encourage people to greatness, and show them they, and everyone else, have the ability to change the way we live—all of us. The Pay It Forward Foundation started as a simple book idea in 1999 and was subsequently turned into a successful movie starring Kevin Spacey, Helen Hunt, and a young Haley Joel Osment.

From the success of the movie and the book, the Pay It Forward Foundation has grown into a global organization that encourages everyday people to make a difference in their lives, and the lives of those around them, by offering an act of kindness for no other reason than it's the human thing to do.

The founders of the organization believe that a more caring, more forgiving society is one that benefits everyone. I find that hard to argue with.

The simplest ideas offer the greatest scope for change—it's time for us all to start paying it forward. The world, and her children, deserves it.

Danny Brown

Be A Show-Off

Our world is connected like never before. Our parents could only dream of how we can reach others with the click of a button. Our children will be the forebearers of the true social networks. Let's use our connectivity now to set the standards for tomorrow.

If you're on Twitter and you like someone's train of thought, recommend them to your community. If you read a blog that inspires or makes you ask questions, share it with friends and colleagues and join the discussion. If you have something to say yourself that makes you think, say it— we're all listening and we want to hear.

We have the opportunity to help the good and the great rise to the challenges ahead. Our leaders can't do everything themselves—we need to be leaders as well. Show off the words and the work of those who inspire you, and in turn you'll inspire others to learn from you.

Ours is a small world in a vast landscape. It's up to you— to *us*—how it stands out in that landscape.

Danny Brown

Human Investment

I was speaking to a friend recently, and we got to chatting about charities and how supporters are almost like investors along the lines of venture capitalists, or stocks and shares guys.

Yet these supporters are much more than a standard investor—as well as donations, they invest time, resources, energy, and much more into the charity they believe in.

Basically, if you're a charity, they invest in *you.*

But this doesn't need to be landlocked into charities. There are many other ways people are investing in you every minute, every hour, every day, and beyond.

It could be they're reading and commenting on your blog. It could be they're conversing with you on Twitter. It could be they're offering advice via email or a phone call. It could be they're babysitting your kids so you and your partner can have a night to yourself. It could be they're offering free workshops to help you get up to speed on something. It could be they're referring your services to someone.

It could be something as simple as they buy you a beer at the pub after a tough day at work.

It doesn't matter what it is—at the end of the day, they're investing in you. Because they believe in you and they want to show it, in whatever form it takes.

So here's a request. A little mini call-to- action, if you like. Think of all the exchanges, conversations, get-togethers, and other connections you've enjoyed over the past week

Danny Brown

(you can make it longer if you like—it's really up to you). Make a note of what these were and who they were with. Think how you can return that investment—a quick thank you call, recognition of a blog comment or tweet, dinner, the promise that they can contact you anytime for any help they might need, a trip to the movies... basically anything you feel merits their investment.

Do this, but do this without looking for anything in return. Do it because you're proud and touched to be part of someone's investment. Do it because *you* want to invest in *them*.

Sound fair?

92

This Thing We Call Humanity

Every day, when I commute to work, there's a mother and son who get on the bus going to the train station. The mother must be in her late fifties, and her son looks as if he's maybe thirty. He clearly has a learning disability, and the mother looks like she's known no other life apart from taking care of her son.

He asks non-stop questions the way a child would to satisfy their curiosity. He sometimes gets agitated, and she rubs his back and holds his hand while answering.

Sitting there, watching them, I'm always touched by the life his mother gave up (and I mean that in the most sincere way), to look after her son and ensure he never feels alone, or lost.

When there's such unconditional love like that, and the choice to give up your own life to make that of another less daunting—*that's* when I know this thing we call humanity, and being better people for all, is not a pipe dream.

Danny Brown

Why We Should Make
More of What We Do An Experience

In 2001, I went backpacking around the West Coast of Australia for six months. I was 33 at the time.

This wasn't a journey that I had to take to "find myself". Instead, it was about taking the time to make an experience. I'd been telling myself since I was 19 that I was going to go backpacking, but never did it.

Coming out of a relationship at the time, and with no ties to bind me, I thought, *"What the heck—I'm going to do this before I get much older."*

So I did. And it was everything I expected and more.

I stayed away from the typical tourist traps and roads, and used my connections to explore the best places for people who wanted to live life and experience it at the pace it was meant to be experienced.

For six glorious months, I probably interacted with less than 30 people.

I was able to look at night skies and enjoy what they're meant to look like, versus the smog-ridden versions we have today. I was able to swim, fish, camp, break a couple of (minor) bones, and feel what life is like when you want to experience it, versus existing in it.

I wonder why we don't do more of that today.

Danny Brown

Life Moves Pretty Fast

In his 1986 classic *Ferris Bueller's Day Off,* director John Hughes shared one fantastic day in the life of uber-school kid, Ferris Bueller. The movie delivers a great line from the title character early on:

"Life moves pretty fast. If you don't stop and look around once in a while, you could miss it."

From that premise, the movie follows Ferris, his best friend, Cameron, and his girlfriend, Sloane as they skip school and take a trip around Chicago. Among many stand out-moments is a scene when the three end up at the Art Institute of Chicago.

As life goes on around him, and Ferris and Sloane catch a quiet place to kiss, Cameron finds himself in front of artist George Seraut's *A Sunday Afternoon on the Island of La Grande Jatte.*

The overriding message in this scene is one of living an experience. In an interview, Hughes explained the inclusion of the museum scene as an opportunity to revisit a place of refuge when he was younger, and share what made him who he was today.

It's this feeling of escape from all the issues Cameron has in his relationship with his father, and where he sees himself in life, that makes this particular scene such an experience in the movie—at that moment, we feel Cameron's solitude, his hopes, his fears, his *life.*

While we may not follow the same path as Ferris and his companions in experiencing one crazy day in Chicago (and if you've never seen the movie, get out and find it now!) we should be making experiences every single day.

The Fallacy of Too Busy

Of course, anytime you mention taking the time to make an experience, there's always the usual push-back:

"I'm too busy."

"I don't have time as it is."

"I can't afford to do that."

"That doesn't sound like me."

None of them are real reasons. They're excuses based around the fallacy of being too busy.

My wife made a great point to me the other week when I said I wanted to work out and get healthier, but I just don't have the time.

My commute sees me travel four hours every day, and so when I get home it's usually play with kids, have dinner, play with kids some more, put kids to bed, spend some time with my wife, and then have my own time to do stuff. At which point sleep is usually a persuasive friend.

So, yes, I'm too busy. *Except I'm not.*

As my wife pointed out, if I really wanted to, I could make exercising part of playtime with my kids. We have a cool little leg workout machine where you stand on two "steps" and move your legs apart and back in on rollers. I could do that while my kids count the steps, and maybe even throw things back and forth at each other.

I could sit at my desk and use the little arm and wrist workout thing my wife has, while reading blog posts I want to catch up on, or when watching Netflix with the kids.

There are many other things I could do—I simply choose not to, through the belief that I don't have time to do it. It doesn't even cost any money—we have the equipment, it's not as if I need to pay gym fees to be healthier.

So, yes—all the reasons we give to' not do' are pretty much meaningless. It's just we don't want to admit as much, because that would mean we need to have *experiences.*

Danny Brown

The World Doesn't Know Us

Another reason we don't want to try to experience life more, and have moments that last a lifetime, is the Fear of Missing Out syndrome, or FOMO.

We believe that if we take a day from life's everyday humdrum, and do something for us, we'll miss something important. Someone else will get that promotion we're after, someone else will get that special deal we're after, someone else will steal the girl or boy our hearts are after.

In short, *someone else* will do something or gain something that should have been *ours*, because we weren't there.

But let's think about this and compare.

Someone else gets that promotion because they're more qualified. The extra stress that promotion would have brought you because you weren't ready isn't there, and your health and relationships are better because of it.

Someone else got that special deal you were after. So what—did you really need that thing that was so specially priced, or were you buying it because the price *told* you that you needed it, as opposed to *truly* needing it?

Someone stole the target of your affection's heart before you. This sucks. I've had this happen many times. But then I thought, *if I was so right for that person, why wasn't the feeling mutual?* Love-filled hearts are two-way—did you really miss out?

We often have such an important view of our place in the world, and yet we don't take any time to actually make ourselves a part of that same world.

We tweet, we post updates on Facebook, we make Vines of how cool our lives are, we Instagram perfectly-caught moments in time—and yet they're more often than not a vision of who we wish we were.

If they are truly how we are, why does Instagram have so

many filters to get our picture in a perfect light?

We have an inane fear of missing out through not being where we need to be (or so we believe), but in reality it's *us* who's missing out on the world.

Add Flavour, Savour, and Enjoy

This year, my son turned five. *Five.*

I have no idea how he got there so fast. I was watching some old YouTube videos of him when he was my daughter's age (she's three), and it struck me how quickly the time has passed between then and now.

Then, he was a stumbling, finding-his-balance, not-quite-baby-but-not-quite-little-boy. Now, he's a confident little boy who doesn't seem so little.

He has great friends and play dates. He gets dressed himself. He can get his own breakfast. He knows how to switch on the Xbox One and work it with voice-commands. Simply put, he's independent and thinks for himself.

Yes, he still needs Mummy and Daddy for the important things, but he's his own little person. And it's great to see.

It's also a reminder that these halcyon years will soon be gone, and, while they'll be replaced with new memories and experiences, the ones we can create now shouldn't be put off.

The email I'm crafting can wait to give a hug. The image I'm searching for for a blog post can wait for kick ball. The cleaning I'm going to do can wait until after the trip to the park while the weather allows. The newspaper can wait and be replaced by sitting on the sofa reading books.

All these little experiences we can make now. And not just little ones. We can take a train trip, draw silly pictures on our driveway, make a project out of the backyard where the kids can build their very own play area to their liking.

We can build memories.

Even for ourselves, we can do this.

We can hold our loved one's hand for the simple act of doing so connects us.

We can smile at a stranger for the simple reason warmth is better than blindness.

We can sit on a hill, close our eyes, and enjoy the breeze on our face.

We can make a meal we've never made before , ruin it, and smile at the failure, because who cares?

We're building memories. We can add flavour to these memories to make them uniquely us, and we can savour them for as long as it takes to satiate us. We can experience what it actually means to *be*, versus the belief of what's meant to be.

We just need to slow down to see where that experience begins.

The Moments We Do Not Take

In May 2014, I almost killed my beautiful little two-year-old girl. It doesn't matter that it was an accident and that she escaped relatively unscathed—the fact of the matter is, had fate chosen to respond just one percent differently, Salem wouldn't be here.

Instead of writing this chapter as a potential catharsis, this page would probably be blank, as would all the other pages that are in this book.

The fact that this page isn't blank does offer me some minor relief—after all, it means she's alive and well—but it also stands as a major reminder that while we may create many moments to cherish, there are just as many we do not take.

The Accident

With Salem turned two in February of that same year, the question of when she should have her first haircut popped up. My wife was dead set against the idea of any haircut then (and Salem has beautiful curly locks, so I can see why), but I'd heard that if you cut (or at least trim) a little girl's hair when it's super curly, then it grows out even more beautifully.

Given that Ewan, our then four-year-old son, had a regular monthly haircut, we decided to take Salem along for her first haircut on one of Ewan's scheduled appointments. After all, he was the seasoned pro—he'd look after his sister.

The haircut turned out great—Salem was a trooper, sat perfectly politely, enjoyed watching cartoons, and passed her first haircut "ordeal" with flying colours. She even sat for a mini-manicure as a treat for good behaviour. That was the great part of the day.

On our way home, we (as per usual) carried both kids on our shoulders—my wife had Ewan, I had Salem. As we walked onto our street, for some reason, Ewan got spooked, and didn't want to be on his mum's shoulders.

I walked over to my wife and son, looked at Ewan and asked what was wrong, since this wasn't like him—he loved shoulder rides. He replied that he was scared and wanted down. So I did what any parent would—I nodded and reached out to get my son down.

All while forgetting I had my daughter on my shoulders.

The moment I reached out for Ewan, I knew something was wrong—the lack of body weight on my shoulders told me I had made a huge mistake, and my daughter was the one about to suffer for it.

I felt the thump at the same time I spun around, and my eyes connected the thump to seeing my daughter hit the ground after falling five and a half feet—twice her height—to hard concrete.

My brain told me she had fallen as "safe" as she possibly could have—straight down in a sitting position, as opposed to tumbling backward head-first—but my eyes saw the head bounce off the concrete as Salem fell back after landing, and immediately battled my brain for the truth.

Whatever the truth was, Salem screamed and started crying. Later, I would find out this was a very good thing, but at that moment in time, all I could think was I had hurt my daughter, and I had to fix that.

The Fear

My wife was still holding Ewan, but lowered him to the ground as I dropped like a dead weight to our daughter, who was crying uncontrollably on the ground. I swept her up and let my wife take her so I could inspect the back of her head.

Fear of a cracked skull, or worse, ran through me as I looked for breaks in the skin, contusions, and every other thing you hear about on TV but don't have a clue about until you wish you did.

While she did have some grazing and the start of a nasty bump, it seemed as though—outwardly—Salem was okay. As I finished checking her head, she turned in my wife's arms and reached out for me, still crying, still being brave.

I took her and told my wife we needed to get her to a hospital to have her checked out, and raced ahead to our home with Salem in my arms, cradling her, soothing her, apologizing to her, kissing her—all the while wishing I was on the phone to get her to the hospital.

The screaming was scary—I didn't know if she'd had internal injuries to her head, and they were making her scream. You hear the horror stories of brains swelling with head injuries, and you don't know that's the case until it's too late.

Every worst thing you can imagine about head injuries went through my mind as we travelled to the emergency ward. Even when we had the X-ray results showing Salem was fine, just s very minor concussion and some bruising, I still wondered if I had caused long-term damage. I still do.

I guess that's what's called *the aftermath*.

The Recovery

Even though Salem had been passed "fit" internally, externally the pain was evident. We couldn't lie her down on her head—or at least with the back of her head down—for a couple of weeks. She'd scream anytime her skull touched a pillow.

I'd sleep on the floor of Salem's room, with her resting on my outstretched arm, keeping her head off the floor as she lay on her side. My wife would sleep on the sofa in our home's grand room, buffering Salem's head, and making sure Salem slept soundly with the protected snuggle mothers do so well.

It took a while, but eventually Salem slept on her own, with the back of her head on the pillow. That was a big step.

Big steps continued. While we haven't had any of the kids on our shoulders since the accident, Salem does feel safe when we lift her up and hoist her in the air only to lower her quickly, to give her a feeling of weightlessness. She giggles at that.

While she still holds on a lot tighter to both my wife and I when we lift her up, she does let us swing her through the air more than she did a few months ago. And she giggles.

For all intents and purposes, Salem has recovered from that almost-oh-so-different moment in 2014. I should ask her what her secret is.

Reactions and Realizations

Since that day, I've run through the same scenario countless times, with many, many different outcomes. Sometimes I play these scenarios out in daylight; more often than not, I awake from a perspiration-filled nightmare, where the graphic images of how different that day could have been fill the place where sleep should be:

- if she'd landed on her head instead of her padded pants;

- if she'd twisted downward instead of falling straight;
- if she hadn't screamed immediately, but fell and remained deathly silent when she hit the ground (a scream means no major damage—silence means something many times worse).

Even though my wife drums into me that it was an accident, and even though Salem's beautiful happy face is in our lives versus so many other outcomes that could have been the very real result, I still have almost daily nightmares.

While the nightmares are the recurring guest of a trip I'd rather forget, they remind me of the moments we do not take, and encourage me to make moments that *are* taken.

I could have lost my daughter shortly after her second birthday. While I have many wonderful pictures and videos of Salem since her birth, they're a fraction of what should be recorded for future family dinners. That changed on May 7, 2014.

I've always said my family is the number one priority in my life. Almost losing Salem showed me how fragile that goal is, and how we all need to grasp at these kinds of goals whenever we have the chance.

We're faced with choices every day:

Do we really need to take that late afternoon meeting that means we won't be home to see our kids go to sleep?

Do we really need to text our friends when we're out with our family at the park or at a dinner?

Do we really need to say "in a minute" when just one minute with our kids will make them smile for the rest of the day?

Do we really need to do anything that isn't a matter of life and death at that moment in lieu of time with our loved ones?

In the grand scheme of things, we're on this pale blue dot we call home for the shortest of time. Yet, we have so many opportunities to create moments that will last a lifetime, and beyond.

Danny Brown

Grab onto these moments. Grab them hard and don't let go because you never know when these moments will become the ones we can never make again.

Because You Matter

When you start a new adventure, it can be pretty daunting. A new job, a new romance, a new school or college. Online is no different.

The first time you join Twitter, it's like a crazy maze. When you log into Facebook, there's no quick set-up guide. If you want to start a blog, the choices can be bewildering.

Then you look around you and see others that are seemingly way ahead of you. People that have 50,000 followers on Twitter, 2,000 friends on Facebook, are in 30,000 Google+ Circles, have 10,000 subscribers to their blog. You begin to doubt whether you should even be here—how can you possibly compare with that?

Don't worry—you can't. But you don't have to. You just need to be you. No one else, just you.

Think about that person on Twitter with 50,000 followers. Did they join the service with 50,000 ready-made followers? No—they started with a clean sheet. Zero. And they built. Through seeing how Twitter worked, how to converse, how to *connect*. But a lot of it was trial and error—much like yours will be, and everyone else's was.

The 2,000 friends on Facebook? Some may be business contacts, some may be personal friends, some may be old school buddies. Some may even be part of the 50,000 Twitter connections. But again, it starts from zero. Just like you will, and we all did.

The 30,000 Circles on Google+? How many are actually

interacting, or sharing, or plussing?

The blogger with 10,000 subscribers? With a bunch of comments on every post? With lots of social bookmarks? That all started somewhere. It went through months of no one reading, or commenting. It takes time to build a community of readers and commenters. But build it, you will.

Because *you* matter, and you're building something special without even knowing it.

That single tweet of yours that someone saw? That made them stop and think, and you mattered to them. That Facebook status update of yours that a mutually connected friend saw and shared with his or her friends? *That* made them stop and think, and you mattered to them.

That blog post you wrote that a complete stranger left a comment about, thanking you for sharing just what they needed at that time? That mattered—all because you wrote something that might be missed by everyone else, but for that one person *you mattered*.

We spend so much time wondering how we can be like someone else. How we can have that person's success. But you know what? There is absolutely nothing wrong with who *you* are. Right here. Right now.

Because at this very moment in time, for someone, somewhere, you matter. And that's all that *really* matters.

Why You Need to Be
the Bane of the Status Quo

We fall into comfort zones easily. We see something that works, or appears to be working, and we settle for that.

It's understandable. After all, experimentation isn't always fun. It can be hard work. It can backfire—results are never guaranteed.

Compare that to the safe and the tried, where we know something has been proven to be successful (relatively or otherwise), and you can see why comfort zones are easier to be a part of.

The thing is, though, comfort zones make us lazy. They confine us and inhibit continued learning. Once we stop learning, we stop living. Maybe not physically, but certainly mentally.

Once the learning disappears, so does the ask. And humans were built to ask.

It's what's helped us grow and evolve to where we are today: seeing something new and not taking it at face value, but asking why it's better, or why we should even care, since the status quo has got us this far.

So if we were built to ask, why do so many of us feel afraid to do so?

If we want someone to work with us, why do we always go for the soft approach as opposed to giving hard reasons why someone *should* work with us?

Why do we fear asking that pretty girl or good-looking guy out, when the worst they can say is no?

Why do we willingly work the craziest hours under the sun, knowing our value is so much more than we're being paid, yet never ask for that meeting to discuss being paid for our worth?

In short, why do we accept, rather than ask?

Isn't it about time we reversed that and ask instead of accept?

Redefining Ordinary
(Or Why It's Okay to Dream Small)

Sometimes, in business and in our personal lives, we wait for the extraordinary to appear before we make a move.

We wait for that one killer application or solution that will take us from Brand X to Brand Everyone Wants a Piece Of. We close doors on ordinary ideas because only extraordinary will sell.

But what defines ordinary?

Cancer research takes ordinary science and medicine and tries to offer extraordinary life-changing results.

While we have digital tools to write our missives, it's still the ordinary pen that's used for our most personal thoughts—thoughts that have the potential to turn the world on its head if we share them.

What we see as extraordinary when it comes to heart transplants, surgeons see as another ordinary day.

An electric bike might be ordinary to our kids, but a tribal member in the most hidden reaches of the jungle could see it as an extraordinary gift from the gods.

Sure, we need to be smart in business. We need to know our decisions will keep a roof over our heads and that of our employees, and put food on our tables.

But you know—sometimes the most ordinary decisions and ideas could be the ones that bring the most extraordinary results.

How are *you* defining ordinary?

Danny Brown

Freedom to Be

When I think back to how I got to where I am today, I see a lot of paths that have been taken.

I see a schoolboy who was incredibly fortunate to have a wonderful education at an amazing school that accepted children for brains as well as financial clout.

I see a teenager at high school who was able to choose the subjects he liked, as opposed to the subjects his parents thought he should take or his teachers wanted him to take.

I see a young man that left home at 19 and moved hundreds of miles away from his family to start a career path that would lead him to this place, right here, right now.

I see the moments that changed his life and led him to another country, another continent, and where he had the support to be who he wanted to be.

In short, I see a lot of good fortune and encouragement.

But I also see one overarching reason for anything that has happened, and anything that will—the power of freedom.

Freedom to make the choices that shaped me and the lives of those around me, whether they be right choices or otherwise.

Freedom to live lives that we choose to live as opposed to lives that would be chosen for us.

Freedom to disagree and be disagreed with.

Simply put, freedom to be.

Freedom is a blessing—make sure you're using it to its fullest.

Danny Brown

Balancing Your Autobiography

In everything we do, and with everyone we know, we're always battling some kind of balancing act.

Finances versus wants and needs, further education versus joining the workforce, overtime at work versus time with our families.

Sometimes we make the right decisions, sometimes we don't.

This is just as true with our online personas and how we portray ourselves in our interaction with others.

Whether it's on Twitter, via our blog, on Facebook, or otherwise, what we do and say defines us.

Sure, we want to share a bit of ourselves and show people we're worth knowing—that's only human.

Getting the balance right is a precarious thing.

Broadcast too much and your worth diminishes. Converse too little and you might never find the people you need to share your message with.

Getting the mix right is tough; presuming you've got it right isn't a guarantee that you have.

A wise friend once told me, "People bring their autobiography with them to every conversation."

The trick is in making sure people want to read it.

Danny Brown

How We Decide
Defines How We Move Forward

People get easily distracted. We see something that gives us the *oooh* ripple of excitement, and we buy into the premise.

For a while, everything is good. We see only positives, and (in hindsight) ignore the questionable.

Then, the cracks appear.

Faults that had always been present start to become clearer. Actions and non-actions reveal a side that we had previously ignored but can't be ignored any longer.

We start to ask the questions that should have been asked from the start. The reactions of the questioned tell us a lot about what our own next steps are.

Do we continue the relationships? Do we accept the faults? Do we look at workarounds? Do we bite the bullet and wait for things to improve?

Or do we cut the ties and accept it was good while it lasted, but some things weren't meant to be?

Questions and decisions are an everyday part of our lives, personally and professionally. Some are easy to answer; others, not so much.

How we decide defines how we move forward. Decide right, and we continue to grow. Decide wrong, and we often never recover.

Are you making the right decisions for you?

Danny Brown

The Power of Oblivious

Every morning, I jump on the train to commute to work, and this includes using the subway when I hit downtown Toronto.

Every morning, without fail, I look around and see faces buried in phones. What the owners of the phones are doing, who knows?

It may be important—a sales presentation in need of fine-tuning before a make-or-break meeting. Or an email response to a social media crisis. Or, perhaps, texting a friend or loved one.

More often than not, people are playing one of the many addictive games that sucker us in and turn us into heads-down zombies.

I get it. Our lives are super busy. We need to be always on, always connected, always doing something. Because busy is *good*, right? Maybe not.

When I look around and see the tops of everyone's heads, it makes me sad.

We have a beautiful world around us. At the time of day I commute to work in the morning, the sun is beginning to rise. In Canadian winters, this is an amazing sight, with whispers of colour trading space with newborn clouds and flickering daylight.

But this is missed for the sake of another minute with eyes glued to a five-inch screen. Or at least it's missed by the majority of people.

Because as I looked around, a young schoolgirl, aged around 15 (I guess) got on the subway and ran up to a similarly-aged young schoolboy, put her arms around him and kissed him, before they turned and just watched the world go by.

Two kids that, for that moment, became oblivious to everything except each other and the wonder of that moment.

The world is a busy place, and more often than not, we need to be busy in it to keep up. But we also need to remember the world will go on being busy long after we've left it.

Perhaps we need to heed the lesson of two young and oblivious kids a little bit more, before the only thing we have left to be oblivious to is breathing.

On Being a Better Person

When I was younger, I did some horrible things. Some, I didn't know better because of age.

At least, I'd like to think so. For example, when I was four years old, I threw a tantrum while shopping with my pregnant mother. As she told me off, I punched her in the stomach.

Now, I'd like to think a four-year-old kid doesn't throw a mean punch, and my mum didn't flinch or give the impression that I'd hurt her. But every time I think of that moment, I think what an idiot thing to do.

Four months later, my sister was born. Early in her childhood, she developed kidney problems. One of them failed to work properly, so she had to take medication for a good chunk of her early years.

The doctors and my mum assured me it wasn't the result of my punch during her pregnancy—but then, they would say that to a little boy, right? So, I always feel I attributed to my sister's health issues.

Skip forward a few years, to when I was maybe 11 or 12 years old; I was a parent's nightmare.

Danny Brown

Early Trials

I lied. Often. I blamed my sister. Often. I stole from my mother's purse, even though we were so poor our daily diet for about five years was nothing but Corn Flakes.

It got so bad that my mum and her boyfriend at the time—soon to be step-dad—sat me down at the kitchen table and threw about £6.50 in loose change—pennies, two pence pieces, ten pence pieces (UK money)—onto a plate in front of me.

He said, "Go on—eat that. That's all we have left for a week because you keep taking everything else. We can't buy food, but we don't want you to starve, so take that." My mum was in tears, and so was I. Had I really become this person?

Clearly, I had. Less than a week later, I stole from my mum's purse again. This time, it was my mum who took action and marched me down to the local police station and had the desk sergeant talk to me.

That worked. It scared the shit out of me on two levels. First, jail scared me. Just being near the cells made me a quivering wreck. Second, it was my mum who marched me down. The woman who always forgave me and saw no wrong in me, despite the fact there was.

That jolted me more than anything and made me realize something had to give.

Thankfully, something did give.

The Finding of Respect

One of my school friends told me about the Army Cadets—an institution for kids 13-18 to learn about army life, go on expeditions and, best of all, fire real guns! As a 12-year-old needing something to keep him busy, I was sold.

Little did I know how much the idea of "being in the army" would change my life.

I found people that wanted to help. I found a sense of belonging. Of loyalty. Of wanting to do right. I found discipline, and honour, and respect for both peers and elders.

Simply put, I found what it's like to be a real member of society.

It took my life on a completely different path than the one I know I would have been on otherwise. From my time in the cadets, I took away what it means to be a member of the community. Of how to stand up for your friends and protect the vulnerable.

That led to me to taking up martial arts and the discipline of karate. Again, I loved the loyalty and peer respect that discipline brings. I studied up until my brown belt, which is one below the black belt, before life events took precedent, and I had to stop training for the next belt.

What karate taught me is that everyone is equal; the concept of "I'm more skilled than you" doesn't exist because there is always the moment someone less experienced can take you by surprise.

Karate also taught me to be a more patient and receptive person, and to accept that situations are never truly in your control—it's how you react that makes the difference.

It also showed me—finally—why we need to continuously strive to be a better person.

The Family is Everything

I truly believe that had I not made the decisions at that turning point, when my mum took me down to the police station, I wouldn't be where I am today.

I wouldn't be the kind of husband I want to be for my wife, nor the father I want to be for my kids, nor the kind of friend I want to be for those that are kind enough to take me on as a friend.

For me, true friends *are* family. I want to be able to act if

I need to in order to protect them and help them when they need help.

I don't always get it right. I still make some crap decisions, and I know it hurts people. But that's the thing with trying to be better than you are—you do make mistakes, and you will continue to do so. The hope is, you learn from them.

You can say all the stuff in the world about how good you are and how you'll look out for those around you.

But if your actions don't back up your words, you'll never be anything other than the person that said so much and delivered so little.

We don't have to be that person. We *shouldn't* be that person. Whether we are or not, though, comes down to one simple question:

Do you want to be a better person, truly?

The rest is up to you.

Be You

Be fearless.
Be bold.
Be new.
Be exciting.
Be inspired.
Be passionate.
Be crazy.

The world is full of normality but who wants to stop at the world?

Be fearless.
Be you.

About the Author

Danny Brown describes himself as a husband, father, optimist, and pragmatist (sometimes in that order). He's a purveyor of not settling for the status quo and never says no to a good single malt.

His last book, *Influence Marketing*, was described as one of the Top 100 Business Books in the US by Nielsen Bookscan. *The Little Book of Inspiration* is his first business book. To read more from Danny, please visit: www.dannybrown.me.

CPSIA information can be obtained
at www.ICGtesting.com
Printed in the USA
LVOW05s0112030616

491026LV00016B/107/P

9 781928 133704